Vikings For Kids

An Enthralling Overview of the Viking Age

Table of Contents

INTRODUCTION

When you hear the word "Vikings," what is the first thing you think of? The professional Minnesota football team? Maybe a television show or a movie? Do you picture blonde warriors with long, flowing hair and horned helmets?

The ancient Vikings lived over one thousand years ago. They have a reputation for being brutal and violent, which makes sense since they were known for raiding and pillaging villages. Their Viking longships struck terror into the hearts of their enemies. The ancient Viking warriors wielded mighty weapons, like long swords and battleaxes, but they were also farmers, craftsmen, and fishermen.

In this book, you'll read surprising facts about the ancient Vikings. Learn about their travels, their daily life, and their ships and weapons. What prompted their passion for adventure? What drove them across seas and oceans? Travel back through the centuries and discover for yourself how these people lived. You'll read about their homes, what they wore, and what they ate.

So, let's get started. See for yourself where these ancient Vikings came from and who they really were. By the time you've finished this book, you'll have a greater understanding of these mighty people.

The ancient Vikings lived over a thousand years ago. They were also called Norsemen or Northmen because they came from the northern countries of Europe.

Today, this region of northern Europe is called **Scandinavia** (*skan-duh-nave-ee-ah*). It includes the countries of Norway, Denmark, and Sweden. Though they lived long ago, the history of the ancient Vikings lives on today. Their legends and stories are seen in movies and television shows. Vikings can even be found in comic books!

The Vikings

Scandinavia has many lakes, rivers, and coastlines. The Vikings were excellent sailors. They built strong wooden ships called *longships* that helped them travel across the seas to explore, trade, and sometimes raid.

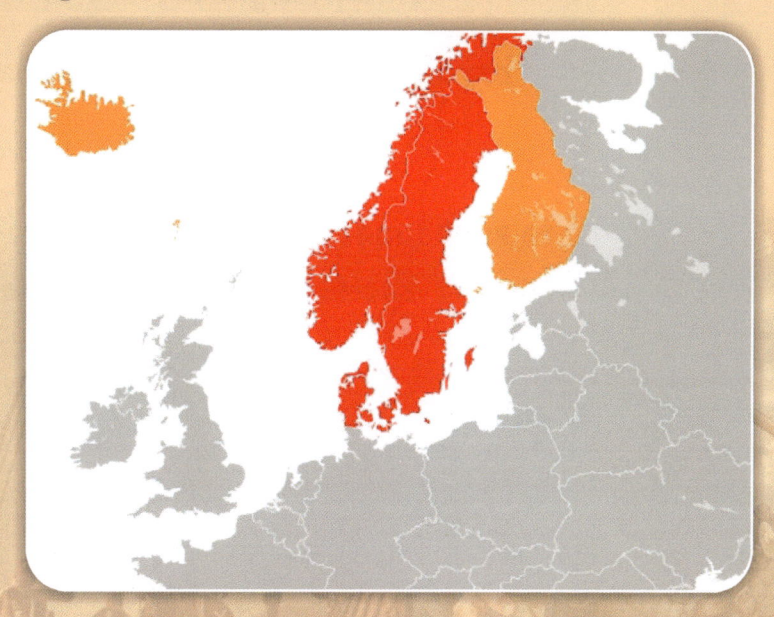

Present-day Scandinavia. This map includes Iceland and the Faroe Islands, which are sometimes included in the definition of Scandinavia.[1]

The word "Viking" comes from an old Norse word that means "pirate" or "raider," but not all Vikings were warriors. Many were farmers, shipbuilders, and traders. They grew crops, raised animals, and made tools, jewelry, and clothes. Life in Scandinavia could be tough. Some land wasn't good for farming, so Vikings often sailed to new places looking for better land and new opportunities.

Viking ships reached faraway places. They sailed to countries in Europe, parts of the Middle East, and even into what is now Russia by using rivers. Some Vikings even crossed the Atlantic Ocean! A Viking explorer named Leif Erikson reached North America around the year 1000. Leif Erikson explored North America almost five hundred years before Christopher Columbus!

Leif Erikson.[2]

Sometimes, Vikings raided towns and monasteries. They surprised people with their fast ships and strong fighting skills. This made them feared in many places. But they were also known for trading. They brought fur, honey, and other goods to trade for things they couldn't make at home, like silver, silk, and spices.

The Vikings were more than fighters—they were explorers, builders, and storytellers. They believed in powerful gods like Thor and Odin. They told exciting stories about the adventures of the gods.

FUN FACT

" Most Vikings were not warriors. Many lived peaceful lives as farmers and craftspeople. "

Prow of a Viking ship.[3]

Today, we can still learn about the Vikings from old writings, ancient ruins, and the stories passed down through time. Movies and TV shows usually show Vikings as wild and fierce. Is there any truth to that?

Rumors About the Vikings

People have been telling stories about the Vikings for hundreds of years. Some of those stories are true, but others are just myths made up to make the Vikings sound more exciting. Let's take a closer look at some of the most common things people say about Vikings and find out what is really true.

Did Vikings wear horned helmets?

Ancient Viking helmet.[4]

FUN FACT

" Only a few Viking helmets have ever been found. They are all pretty plain and practical. "

It's a fun idea, but it's not true. Real Viking helmets did not have horns. Those fancy horned helmets you see in cartoons or costumes would have been a bad idea in battle. An enemy could grab them too easily. Vikings wore simple helmets made of iron to protect their heads. They were designed for fighting, not for show.

Did Viking warriors have long hair?

Not always. Some did, but long hair could be a problem in a fight. Long hair is easy to grab. Viking warriors probably kept their hair shorter or tied it back when they were going on raids.

FUN FACT

> "Viking hairstyles weren't all the same. Some Vikings liked neat looks, while others might have preferred something messier."

Did Vikings care about how they looked?

They sure did. Even though they were tough and spent a lot of time outdoors or at sea, Vikings liked to stay clean. Archaeologists have found combs, razors, and tweezers in Viking sites, so we know they took care of their hair and beards. They probably bathed more often than a lot of people in Europe at the time.

Did Vikings send their dead off in burning boats?

That's one of the most famous Viking myths, but it didn't happen very often. Some important people were buried in ships, but the ships usually stayed on land and were covered with dirt and stones. The idea of a flaming ship floating into the sunset looks great in movies, but it wasn't the usual way Vikings honored their dead.

Were all Viking men warriors?

No. Most Viking men were farmers. They spent their days growing crops, taking care of animals, and building things. Only a small group went on raids, and even they were usually home most of the year. They had to tend to their land like everyone else.

Did the Vikings work together?

Not really. Vikings came from different parts of Scandinavia, and they often followed local chiefs. They even fought each other over land and power. Vikings weren't one big group. They consisted of lots of small communities.

Ancient Viking swords.[5]

Did Viking women fight as warriors?

Most Viking warriors were men, but there is evidence that some women fought. Old Viking stories talk about brave female fighters called *shieldmaidens*. For a long time, people thought those were just legends. A Viking grave in Sweden had weapons and war gear, and the person buried there turned out to be a woman. So, while it wasn't common, it seems that some Viking women really did go into battle.

Runes

The Vikings didn't use the same kind of alphabet we use today. They spoke a language called Old Norse. When they wanted to write something down, they used symbols called **runes** (*roonz*). Runes were carved into wood, bone, and stone to share messages or to remember someone important.

One of the most interesting things the Vikings left behind was runestones. They are also called picture stones. You can still find some of them standing today out in fields or near old villages.

Stora Hammar stone.[6]

One well-known example is the Stora Hammar stone. It can be found on an island in Sweden called Gotland. If you look closely at it, you'll see carvings of Viking warriors, a longship filled with people, and a big bird that is probably an eagle. Some people think the bird might be a symbol for Odin. He was one of the most important gods in Viking myths. Historians believe the stone was made sometime between the 700s and 800s.

These stones are kind of like storybooks. They don't tell us everything, but they give us clues about what the Vikings believed, what mattered to them, and how they wanted to be remembered. Even though their world looked very different from ours, the Vikings were people with their own stories to tell—just like us.

Fill in the blanks in the statements below to gauge your understanding of the chapter you just read.

1. More Viking men were _____ rather than warriors.

2. Some of the land in _____ was not good for farming.

3. The term "Viking" is believed to have come from the ancient Norse word for _____.

4. The Vikings left carved stones called _____ that told stories about their lives and battles.

5. The Vikings built amazing wooden ships called _____.

Chapter 1 Answers

1. Farmers (or craftsmen or fishermen)

2. Scandinavia

3. Pirate (or raider)

4. Runestones

5. Longships

Vikings didn't have cities like we do today. Instead, they lived in small villages or farms. Different Viking groups could be separated by forests or water. Even so, they were still part of the same culture and shared many of the same beliefs.

Death and Burial

One way we have learned about Viking life is by studying the way they honored their dead. Vikings believed that death wasn't the end. They thought it was the start of a new part of their journey.

Vikings thought that the spirit traveled to another world filled with gods, magical powers, and other spirits. Some people believed that brave warriors who died in battle would go to a great hall called **Valhalla** (*val-hal-uh*), where they'd feast and fight until the end of time. Others believed in different places for different kinds of deaths, like **Fólkvangr** (*fohlk-vahn-gr*). It was ruled by the goddess **Freyja** (*frey-uh*).

To help someone reach the afterlife, Vikings gave them special burials. Sometimes, they were buried with items like tools, jewelry, or even animals. These were things they might need in the next life. A few very important people were even buried in ships. These ships weren't sent out to sea. Instead, they were placed on land and covered with dirt and stones to form a mound. The idea was that the ship would carry the person into the afterlife even without water.

Viking burial mounds in Gamla Uppsala, Sweden.[7]

What about women? Women were very important in Viking society. They helped run farms, manage households, and even held power in some cases. When women died, they were buried with things they used in daily life, like cooking tools, jewelry, or items to make clothing. Some women were buried in large mounds or even in ships. This shows that they were honored and respected.

Storytelling

The Vikings used a language called **Old Norse**. Instead of an alphabet, they had special symbols called *runes*. The letters were made of straight lines, which made them easier to carve into wood, bone, or stone.

A runestone in Sweden.[8]

FUN FACT

"
Most of the time, Vikings wrote runes from left to right, just like we do today. Sometimes, especially on older stones, or for decoration, they switched things up and wrote the next line from right to left. This special style was called boustrophedon (boo-struh-fee-daan). A few runes were even written up and down, but that wasn't common.
"

One of the Jelling stones.[9]

Runestones were sometimes used to tell stories, honor someone who had died, or mark an important event. The Vikings didn't write books the way we do.

Most of their history was passed down by storytellers called *skalds*. These storytellers shared tales of mighty gods, brave warriors, and the creation of the world. Many of these stories were told around fires during the long winter nights. Some were written down later, but for a long time, they were remembered by word of mouth.

Chapter 2 Activity

Decide whether the following statements are true or false.

1. The Vikings never buried their loved ones nearby because they were afraid of ghosts.

2. Viking writing was called hieroglyphics.

3. Storytellers in Viking society were called skalds.

4. The Vikings did not believe in an afterlife.

5. An important person who died was often placed in a longship and buried under dirt and stones.

Chapter 2 Answers

1. False

2. False

3. True

4. False

5. True

What was life like for a Viking family? Let's find out!

Most Viking families lived on small farms. They grew their own food and raised animals like sheep, goats, and cows. Everyone helped out—even kids! Some people lived in villages instead of farms. They used their skills to help the community. Some made cloth and clothes. Others were *blacksmiths*, shaping metal into tools, weapons, and armor.

At first, the Vikings didn't have kings or a unified government. They were ruled by local leaders called *chieftains*. A chieftain helped solve problems, made important decisions, and led others in battle when needed. Later on, by around the 11th century CE, some Viking lands were ruled by kings or *monarchs*. They had more power and ruled over larger areas.

Viking Society

Viking society had different groups of people. These are called *classes*. These were the main three classes:

- ▶ **Nobles** – These were rich and powerful people. Nobles were often warriors or chieftains.
- ▶ **Freedmen** – These were free people like farmers, traders, or blacksmiths. They worked hard and could own land and homes.
- ▶ **Slaves** – Also called thralls, these people were often captured during raids or born into slavery. They had to work for others. They didn't have the same rights as the other classes.

As long as a Viking was free, they had rights. Free people could carry weapons, protect themselves, and speak up at meetings. When big decisions needed to be made, the people would gather together in a meeting called a **Thing** (*ting*). At the Thing, free men could vote and help decide what was best for the community.

Viking families sometimes lived far apart. If there was an attack, they would gather in buildings or small forts for protection. These places were also used for meeting neighbors and trading goods. People came to sell things like tools, clothes, or food. They would buy things they didn't have at home.

What Did the Vikings Wear?

The Vikings didn't wear clothes just to stay warm. They actually cared about how they looked!

Most Viking clothing was made at home by women. They used wool from their sheep. They spun the wool into thread and weaved it into cloth. Some wealthier families also used linen, which was made from flax plants. A few even had pieces of silk they traded for from faraway places.

Men usually wore wool pants called **breeches** (*bri-chiz*) and long tunics that came down past the waist. These tunics were sometimes decorated with colorful embroidery around the sleeves or bottom edge. Men wore leather belts to hold up their pants or carry tools. When it got cold, they put on thick wool cloaks, which they would fasten with a pin or brooch (*broach*—rhymes with coach).

Women wore long linen or wool dresses. Many wore something that looked like an apron over their dress. They held it up with metal brooches on the shoulders. In the winter, they wore fur-lined boots and cloaks to keep warm. Hats made of fur or leather helped protect their heads from the cold.

Common Viking women's and men's clothing.[10]

Even everyday people liked to look nice. Vikings often wore jewelry, like bracelets and armbands made of silver or bronze. Their cloaks and tunics were sometimes fastened with decorative pins or brooches. They traded for shiny things like glass beads and polished stones to make necklaces and other ornaments.

"Vikings liked anything that made them look better! They even made items like combs and tweezers out of bone to help keep themselves clean and tidy. "

Silver Viking bracelets.[11]

Viking Homes

Viking homes were made from whatever materials were available nearby. In some places, people built houses out of wood. In other places, they used stone or even blocks of earth called *turf*. The roofs were often *thatched*, which means they were covered with bundles of straw, reeds, or long grass tied together to keep out rain and snow.

Most Viking families lived in a type of house called a *longhouse*. These were long, one-room buildings with a high roof. Wooden posts helped hold up the roof. In the middle of the room was an open fireplace. This fire was used for cooking food and for keeping the house warm during the winter months. A small hole in the roof let the smoke escape.

FUN FACT

" Everyone in the family ate, worked, and slept in the same big room. In the winter, they sometimes even brought animals, like cows or goats, inside the house to help keep them warm and safe. "

Viking home reconstruction.[12]

A Viking family usually included a mom and dad, their children, and sometimes grandparents, aunts, uncles, and cousins. Family was very important. Vikings looked after one another.

Women had many important jobs. They made clothes by spinning wool into thread and weaving it into cloth. They also cooked, cleaned, and cared for the children. If the men went off to fight or trade, the women took charge of the farm and made sure everything ran smoothly.

Kids had chores too. Boys helped with farming and hunting. Girls helped with cooking, weaving, and other work around the house. Everyone had to pitch in.

A Viking village.[13]

What Did the Vikings Eat?

Vikings had to work hard to get their food, but they had a lot of different things to eat. Many Viking families hunted in the forests for wild animals like deer, elk, and wild boar. In the far north, they also hunted seals, whales, and reindeer.

Vikings raised animals too. They kept pigs, sheep, cows, and even ducks and geese for meat, milk, eggs, and wool. They also fished in rivers and the sea, catching all kinds of fish.

Viking farmers grew grains like barley, oats, rye, and sometimes wheat. These grains were used to make porridge, which was a common breakfast. *Porridge* is kind of like oatmeal. In their gardens, they grew vegetables like cabbage, peas, and onions. They picked berries and wild fruits from the forests.

Viking Warriors and Their Weapons

Not all Viking men were warriors, but some went on long trips to get treasure or goods from other places. These trips sometimes took them far from home. While raids were often violent, some of these trips were more like trading journeys.

Vikings often carried weapons to protect themselves even when they were not at war. Most men, women, and even older kids carried a small knife called a **seax** (*say-ax*). It was useful on the farm or during a hunt.

When Vikings went into battle, they used spears, axes, or

Viking longswords.[14]

swords. Swords were very valuable. Only the richer warriors usually had them. They also carried round wooden shields to protect themselves.

Some stories tell of brave women who also went into battle. These women were called shieldmaidens. Some historians think shieldmaidens might be more legend than fact, but graves have been found where women were buried with weapons. It's possible some Viking women really did fight.

A Viking shieldmaiden.[15]

When Viking warriors attacked, they often used surprise. They moved quickly, striking before people had time to fight back. This helped them win battles and escape before the enemy could stop them.

Chapter 3 Activity

Choose the correct word to fill in the blanks.

1. A female warrior was called a _____.
    (Vikingness/shieldmaiden)

2. A common breakfast for Vikings was_____.
    (Eggs and toast/porridge)

3. A Viking family most commonly lived in a _____.
    (Longhouse/Longboat)

4. Viking men often wore pants known as _____.
    (Breeches/pantaloons)

5. A public Viking meeting was called a _____.
    (Thrall/Thing)

1. Shieldmaiden

2. Porridge

3. Longhouse

4. Breeches

5. Thing

The Vikings believed in many gods and goddesses. They told lots of stories about magical places and powerful beings. One of their most important stories was about a huge tree called **Yggdrasil** (*igg-drah-sil*). They thought this tree held up the whole universe!

1886 sketch of Yggdrasil.[16]

Yggdrasil was a special ash tree. It was so big that it touched the sky and reached deep underground. The Vikings believed that nine different worlds or kingdoms were connected to this tree. These worlds were home to different kinds of beings, like gods, giants, elves, dwarfs, and even people.

An eagle lived at the top of the tree. A dragon named **Nidhogg** (*need-hog*) curled around the roots and tried to chew on them. The tree was so strong that it was believed it would last forever.

Here are the nine worlds the Vikings believed in:

- ▶ A world for the gods, high in the sky.
- ▶ A world for humans where people like the Vikings lived.
- ▶ A cold, dark world for the dead.
- ▶ A hot world full of fire and lava.
- ▶ A land of giants who were enemies of the gods.
- ▶ A bright world for the light elves.
- ▶ A dark world for the dark elves or dwarfs who lived underground.
- ▶ A land for the Vanir gods, who were different from the main gods.
- ▶ A misty world of ice and snow.

FUN FACT

> Vikings didn't have a written language at first, so they passed down these stories by telling them out loud. This is called an oral tradition.

Gods and Goddesses of the Vikings

The Vikings believed in many gods and goddesses, but two of the most famous were *Odin* and *Thor*. You might have seen them in movies and TV shows before!

Odin

Odin (*oh-din*) was one of the most important gods. He was called the All-father because he was like the father of all the gods. He was their leader.

Odin was the god of wisdom, war, magic, and poetry. He had two ravens named **Huginn** (thought) (*hoo-gin*) and Muninn (memory) (*moo-nin*). They flew around the world and

Odin on his throne.[17]

brought him news. Odin also rode a magical horse named **Sleipnir** (*slipe-neer*). His horse had eight legs and could travel anywhere—even to the land of the dead!

Thor

Thor was Odin's son. He was the god of thunder, storms, and strength. He protected both gods and humans from giants. Thor had a magical hammer called **Mjölnir** (*mee-ohl-neer*). When he threw the hammer, it always came back to him. The Vikings believed that when they heard thunder, it was the sound of Thor swinging his hammer in battle.

Painting of Thor fighting giants.[18]

Freyja

Freyja was a powerful goddess. She was known for love, beauty, and battle. She could be kind, but she was also strong and brave. Freyja rode in a chariot pulled by two large cats. Sometimes, she rode a golden boar. She was also connected to a kind of Viking magic called **seidr** (*say-der*). Some warriors hoped to go to Freyja's hall, Fólkvangr, when they died bravely in battle.

Freyja.[19]

Ragnarök – The End of the World

The Vikings believed that one day, the world would end in a huge battle called **Ragnarök** (*rahg-nuh-rohk* or *rag-na-rock*). It would be a fight between the gods and their enemies, like the giants. Odin would lead the gods. Even Thor would fight. Many gods would not survive, and the world would be destroyed by fire and floods. After Ragnarök, a new world would rise. This world would be pure, and life would begin again.

Valhalla

The Vikings believed that when someone died, their spirit went to the afterlife. There were different places a person could go. Where they went depended on how they lived and how they died.

One place was called **Hel** (*hell*). It wasn't a bad place. It was more like a quiet land where people went if they died of old age or sickness. It looked a lot like the world they lived in. People who went there were believed to stay until the end of the world.

But if a person died bravely in battle, they would go somewhere else. The Vikings believed that **Valkyries** (*val-kur-eez*)—fierce warrior women—would come to the battlefield and choose the bravest warriors. These warriors would be taken to **Valhalla** (*val-hall-ah*), the hall of Odin. In Valhalla, they would feast, fight, and celebrate every day while they waited to help the gods in the final battle known as Ragnarök.

Ancient runestone depicting Thor, Odin, and Freyr.[20]

Some Vikings also believed in ghosts, especially the kind that didn't rest peacefully. These ghostly figures were called **draugar** (*drow-gur*). They were thought to come back to scare the living if they had done something wrong or if they had not been properly buried.

Viking Celebrations and Traditions

The Vikings had many celebrations, just like we do today. They celebrated weddings, good harvests, and the birth of children. These events were important to their families and communities.

Before a big feast, the Vikings sometimes made animal sacrifices to their gods. This was called a **blót** (*bloat*). It was a way to say thank you or ask for help from the gods.

Vikings prayed to different gods and goddesses for things that mattered in everyday life. They prayed to gods for good weather, a healthy family, strong animals, and winning battles. They followed special rituals to keep the gods happy.

Some Vikings also honored their *ancestors*—the people who came before them. They believed these family members still watched over them.

Choose the correct answer to the following statements.

1. Odin is often depicted with two ravens. What were their names?

   a. Thor and Loki

   b. Memory and Thought

   c. Strength and Power

2. These often led the souls of the dead who died in battle to the land of Valhalla.

   a. Shieldmaidens

   b. Valkyries

   c. Medicine women

3. What was the great battle against the giants called?

   a. Ragnarök

   b. Stora Hammar

   c. Valhalla

4. What was the name of Thor's hammer?

   a. Thunder

   b. Mjölnir

   c. Lightning

1. B: Memory and Thought

2. B: Valkyries

3. A: Ragnarök

4. B. Mjölnir

The Vikings are well known for being brave explorers and fierce warriors. A long time ago, they began sailing across the sea in strong wooden ships called *longships*. These ships could move fast. They could travel up rivers and across the ocean. Longships had both sails and oars, so they could move with or without the wind.

Lindisfarne Priory ruins.[21]

The earliest Viking raids happened in places like Ireland and Britain. At first, only small groups of Vikings attacked. They moved quickly and surprised people. They often targeted churches and farms.

One of the most famous early raids happened in 793 CE at a monastery in **Lindisfarne** (*lin-diss-farn*) in northern England. The monastery was important to Christians. The attack shocked everyone. It marked the beginning of what we call the *Viking Age*.

As time went on, Viking war bands grew larger and bolder. They began attacking bigger towns and religious centers. They took what they wanted, such as animals, food, weapons, gold, and even people.

The Vikings also settled in many of the places they visited. In Ireland, they built towns along the coast. They used these places to trade and launch more raids. They also raided and settled in parts of Scotland, Wales, and England.

FUN FACT

"Did you know the Vikings founded the city of Dublin in Ireland? Around the year 841 CE, they set up a base there to trade and launch raids. It started as a Viking camp, but it grew into a busy town. Today, it's the capital of Ireland!"

Some Vikings sailed across the English Channel and attacked northern France. France was harder to conquer, but the Vikings were able to settle in one area. This area later became known as Normandy.

Other Viking groups traveled even farther. Vikings from Sweden sailed east across the Baltic Sea into Russia, Ukraine, and other parts of eastern Europe. They followed rivers and traded with people far from their homeland.

Wherever the Vikings went, people feared the sight of their longships. Their reputation as strong and daring warriors made a big impact on Europe.

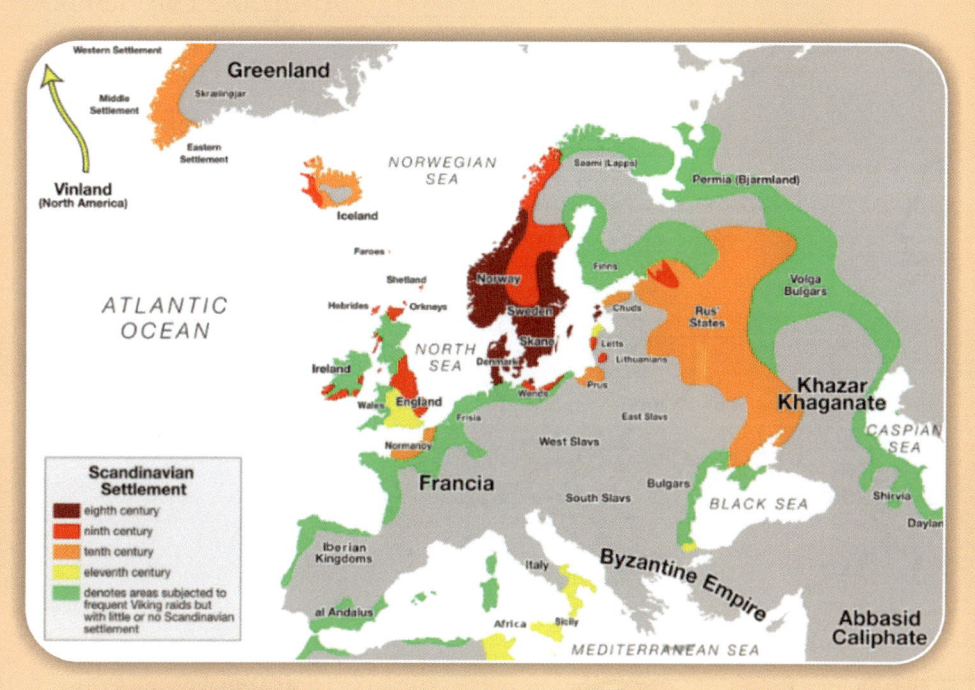

Viking expansion.[22]

The Viking Navy

The Vikings didn't have an organized navy like countries do today. Viking chieftains gathered groups of warriors. They sailed off in their longships to raid other lands.

Sometimes, only a few ships were used for surprise attacks. Other times, they used dozens or even hundreds of ships!

Animal head post from a Viking ship.[23]

The Siege of Paris

One of the most famous Viking attacks was against the city of Paris in what is now France. In 845 CE, a Viking leader named **Reginherus** (*reh-gin-hair-us*) led a large fleet of ships up the **Seine** (*sen*) River. The Vikings had already raided parts of France before, but this attack was much bigger.

FUN FACT

" Some think Reginherus might have been the legendary Ragnar Lothbrok! Stories say Ragnar was a brave warrior, a king, and even a dragon slayer! "

The Vikings reached Paris and surrounded the city. This tactic is called a *siege*. This means they blocked the city. People inside couldn't get food or supplies. The Vikings caused a lot of fear, and they refused to leave unless they were paid.

The king at the time, Charles the Bald, paid the Vikings seven thousand pounds of silver to leave Paris. Paying the Vikings off only encouraged more raids later.

Vikings invade Paris.[24]

The Battle of Hafrsfjord

Not all Viking battles happened far from home. In what we now call Norway, Viking leaders fought each other for power. One powerful chieftain named Harald Fairhair wanted to unite the small kingdoms of Norway into one.

Around 872 CE, Harald fought and won a major battle called the Battle of **Hafrsfjord** (*hahf-rs-fyord*). A little over a decade later, he became the first king of a united Norway.

Harald's son Erik became known as Erik Bloodaxe because he killed several of his brothers to become king. Only one brother Haakon (hoh kawn) survived because he was raised in England.

After Erik's rule, Haakon the Good returned to Norway and became king. He ruled until about 960 CE, when he died in battle.

Battle of Hafrsfjord.[25]

Another Big Attack on Paris

In 885 CE, the Vikings attacked Paris again—this time with even more ships! Some sources say they used nearly seven hundred ships in this massive attack. The people of Paris didn't give up for almost a year. Eventually, they paid the Vikings to make them leave.

Chapter 5 Activity

Can you fill in the blanks below?

1. One of the most well-known Viking raids involved a nearly year-long siege against the city of _____.

2. An early Viking raid against Britain took place around 793 CE against the Lindisfarne _____.

3. The construction of _____ made it easy for the Viking raiding parties to travel so far inland.

4. Some of the earliest raids of the Vikings occurred along the coasts of _____.

5. The Vikings didn't have an organized _____.

1. Paris

2. Monastery

3. Longships

4. Ireland (Britain is also an acceptable answer.)

5. Navy

The Vikings sometimes traveled to trade, and sometimes, they went to raid. But why did they raid in the first place?

They Needed Food

Some parts of Scandinavia had poor soil and short growing seasons. It was hard to grow enough food. When they couldn't farm or trade for food, the Vikings would sometimes raid other places to get what they needed, like meat, grain, and fish.

They Wanted More Land

As Viking families got bigger, they needed more land to grow crops and raise animals. Since there wasn't much good farmland in their own land, they looked for better places in other countries. Sometimes, after raiding, they stayed and built new homes there.

They Wanted Treasure

Vikings liked shiny things like silver, gold, glass beads, and jewelry. They often traded animal furs for these items. If they couldn't trade or didn't have money, they raided villages and took what they wanted.

Viking jewelry.[26]

They Wanted Power

Viking warriors were known for their surprise attacks. This made people afraid of them. The more places they raided, the more powerful they seemed. Their scary reputation helped them win more battles and made it easier to take control of new places.

Berserkers: The Wild Warriors

Some Viking warriors were called **berserkers** (*bur-zur-kers*). They wore bear or wolf skins. They fought with wild fury. People said they were so angry in battle that they could not even be stopped by their own leaders! Some stories say they didn't feel pain and kept fighting until the very end.

Viking towns of Scandinavia.[27]

Fun Facts About Viking Longships

▶ Viking longships were *shallow*. They could sail up rivers and land right on beaches.

▶ Both ends of the ship looked the same. This means the ship could go forward or backward without turning around.

▶ Some longships were as long as seventy-five feet. They could carry thirty to sixty warriors!

Reconstructed Oseberg Viking ship.[28]

Why Did They Keep Going?

The Vikings didn't just raid for food and treasure. They were also curious and loved exploring. They wanted to see what was beyond the oceans and rivers they knew. Over time, their raids helped them discover new places to live and trade.

Even though the Vikings were feared as raiders, they were also great shipbuilders, smart sailors, and brave explorers. They traveled farther than almost anyone else in their time.

Chapter 6 Activity

Decide whether the following statements are true or false.

1. The Vikings were known for their surprise attacks.

2. Viking ships were not able to navigate narrow, shallow rivers.

3. Berserkers wore lion skins into battle.

4. Vikings often raided to find things they could not make or grow in their homeland.

5. Viking longships could move forward and backward without turning around.

Chapter 6 Answers

1. True
2. False
3. False
4. True
5. True

By the 800s CE, Viking raids had grown from small surprise attacks into major invasions. What started as quick raids to grab treasure and supplies soon became larger efforts to conquer and control land. Viking warriors used to return home after a raid, but over time, they began staying in the places they attacked. To hold onto these lands, they built settlements, formed governments, and sometimes even made peace deals with local rulers.

England territory in 878 CE.[29]

The Rise of the Danelaw in England

One of the best-known examples of Viking settlement happened in England. Around 865 CE, a powerful Viking army called the *Great Heathen Army* landed on English shores. This army was led by several Viking chieftains, including the legendary Ivar the Boneless.

Instead of returning home after raiding, these warriors stayed and claimed the land for themselves. Over time, they took control of much of northern and eastern England. The land they ruled became known as the Danelaw because it was governed by Danes from Denmark. In the Danelaw, Viking laws, language, and customs mixed with those of the local people. This left a lasting mark on English history.

Invasions of Britain.[30]

Viking Expansion into Europe and Beyond

After establishing themselves in England, the Vikings continued to explore and expand into other parts of Europe. Some crossed the English Channel and raided into what is known as France. Others traveled east. They journeyed along the Danube and **Dnieper** (*nee-per*) Rivers, sailed across the Black Sea, and even reached parts of what we now call Russia and Ukraine.

Viking voyages.[31]

Rollo the Walker and the Founding of Normandy

One Viking leader named Rollo the Walker became especially famous in France. Around 911 CE, Rollo led Viking raids into the northern part of the country. After years of fighting, the French king decided to make peace with him. Rollo was given land and allowed to rule it if he promised to stop raiding.

This deal marked the beginning of *Normandy*—a Viking territory that got its name from "Northmen." Rollo became the first duke of Normandy. His Viking followers settled the land, married the local people, and became known as the Normans.

FUN FACT

"Rollo's grave can still be visited today in the Cathedral of Rouen, France."

Statue of Rollo.[32]

Oleg the Wise and the Kievan Rus'

In the east, another Viking leader named Oleg the Wise traveled into the lands of the *Slavic peoples*. These were groups who spoke similar languages and lived in parts of what are now Ukraine, Russia, and Belarus.

Around 879 CE, Oleg captured the city of **Kyiv** (*kee-eev*), which became the center of a new kingdom called **Kievan Rus'** (*kee-yiv-an roos*). This kingdom was a mix of Viking and Slavic cultures. It played a big role in the early history of Russia and Ukraine. Oleg became known as a wise and powerful ruler who helped shape this growing kingdom.

Map of Kievan Rus'.[33]

The Discovery of Iceland and Greenland

Around 860 CE, a Viking explorer discovered Iceland by accident while sailing through the North Atlantic. Other Vikings followed his trail. They found Iceland's coasts were great for fishing. Many settled there permanently.

About a hundred years later, another famous Viking, Erik the Red, sailed even farther west. He reached a large, icy land. He called it Greenland even though most of it was covered in ice. Erik hoped the pleasant name would encourage people to move there. In 985 CE, Erik led a group of settlers to Greenland and started a small colony.

Leif Erikson: First European to Reach North America

Erik the Red's son, Leif Erikson, inherited his father's love of adventure. Around the year 1000 CE, Leif sailed west from Greenland. He reached the coast of what is now Canada. He called the place Vinland. Leif might have been the first European to set foot on the continent. He did so nearly five hundred years before Christopher Columbus.

Leif Erikson landing in North America.[34]

Chapter 7 Activity

Draw a line to match the names on the left side to the event, name, or place on the right side.

Leif Erikson	Led the Great Heathen Army
Rollo	Believed to have discovered North America before Christopher Columbus
Ivan the Boneless	Discovered Greenland
Erik the Red	Founder of Kievan Rus'
Oleg the Wise	Created the Duchy of Normandy

Chapter 7 Answers

Leif Erikson – Believed to have discovered North America before Christopher Columbus

Rollo – Created the Duchy of Normandy

Ivan the Boneless – Led the Great Heathen Army

Erik the Red – Discovered Greenland

Oleg the Wise – Founder of Kievan Rus'

The **Varangian** (*vuh-ran-jee-uhn*) **Guard** was a special group of Viking warriors who became *bodyguards* (soldiers who protect important leaders) for the rulers of the Byzantine Empire. This was a powerful kingdom in southeastern Europe. It was centered in what is now the city of Istanbul, Turkey. This city used to be called Constantinople.

Varangians in Russia.[35]

Where Did They Come From?

Many of these Viking guards came from a land called Kievan Rus'. This kingdom was located in what is today Ukraine, Russia, and Belarus.

Remember? It was started by Oleg the Wise and Vikings from Sweden.

The Varangian Guard was first formed around the year 988 CE when Byzantine Emperor Basil II asked Prince Vladimir of Kievan Rus' for help. Basil needed strong, trustworthy fighters to help stop a rebellion. Prince Vladimir sent around six thousand Viking warriors to Constantinople. They were so brave and skilled that Emperor Basil made them his personal guards.

What Did the Varangian Guard Do?

These Viking guards were known for their fierce fighting, loyalty, and strength. Their main job was to protect the emperor and the palace. They promised to defend the ruler with their lives.

Over the years, they fought in many battles for the empire, including in faraway places like Italy and Sicily. In one battle, they helped the empire fight against Arab invaders. In another, they fought the Normans. They were the descendants of Vikings who had settled in France.

The Varangian Guards around the 11th century.[36]

What Did They Look Like?

The Varangians were tall and strong. They wore armor and carried large axes and swords made of iron. Some wore shirts with a dragon symbol to show their bravery. People said they looked scary with their long hair and fierce expressions.

FUN FACT

"Some old stories say that members of the Varangian Guard wore a ruby (a red gemstone) in one ear. That detail is part of a legend. However, that doesn't mean it wasn't true!"

What Does Varangian Mean?

The word Varangian comes from Old Norse. It likely means "sworn companion." They took an oath to protect and serve. The Vikings from Sweden who settled in eastern Europe were also called Rus', a word that might have come from the Norse word for "rowers" because they used boats with oars.

The Varangian Legacy

In the first one hundred years, the Varangian Guard served at least five emperors. They kept guarding the palace for nearly two hundred more years after that!

Over time, more Anglo-Saxon warriors from England joined them, especially after the Norman Conquest in 1066. Many English soldiers lost their homeland and looked for new places to live and fight. By the end of the 1000s, the Varangian Guard included both Vikings and English warriors.

> " The Varangians were paid very well. They were often paid in gold, silver, or jewels. They became some of the highest-paid soldiers in the empire. "

Viking runes discovered in Constantinople.[37]

Did the Vikings Really Leave a Mark?

Yes! You can still find evidence of the Varangian Guard today.

In the ancient church called **Hagia Sophia** (*hah-yuh so-fee-uh*) in Istanbul, Viking warriors carved their names into the stone walls using Viking runes.

In Venice, Italy, there's a marble statue called the **Piraeus** (*pih-ray-us*) **Lion**. It has Viking runes scratched into its shoulder. These carvings tell of Viking warriors who served in the Byzantine Empire long ago.

The Piraeus Lion.[38]

Choose the correct word to fill in the blanks.

1. In Venice, visitors can still see the runes on the statue of _____. (the Piraeus Lion/Leif Erikson)

2. The Vikings of the Varangian Guard mostly acted as the king's _____. (servants/bodyguards)

3. The Varangians were known to wear a _____ in their earlobe. (green emerald/red ruby)

4. The Vikings from Sweden who settled in eastern Europe were called Kievan Rus', which in Old Norse means _____. (fierce warriors/ rowers)

5. Kievan Rus' is believed to have been founded by _____. (Ivan the Boneless/Oleg the Wise)

Chapter 8 Answers

1. The Piraeus Lion
2. Bodyguards
3. Red ruby
4. Rowers
5. Oleg the Wise

Over the centuries, the Vikings sailed across Europe, attacking towns and sometimes staying to live in the lands they raided. They built homes and farms in places like England, Scotland, Ireland, and even parts of France and eastern Europe.

But the time of Viking raids didn't last forever. Why did the Viking Age come to an end?

Stronger Defenses

As time went on, other countries became stronger. They built castles and forts to protect their towns from Viking attacks. These countries also formed larger armies to fight back. Once this happened, the Vikings couldn't attack as easily as before.

The Spread of Christianity

Many Vikings eventually settled in places where people practiced **Christianity** (*kris-chee-an-i-tee*). This religion was followed by most Europeans. In the early days, Vikings followed their own religion. They prayed to many gods and goddesses like Odin and Thor. People who weren't Christian were often called *pagans*.

Vikings and Christians didn't always get along.

Saint Ansgar in Sweden.[39]

Over time, some Viking leaders realized that it was easier to trade and live peacefully with their neighbors if they became Christian too.

Harald Bluetooth and the First Viking Kings

In 960 CE, a Viking leader named **Harald Bluetooth Gormsson** (*gorm-son*) became king of Denmark. Before the Viking lands had official kings, many local leaders were called **magnates** (*mag-nayts*). These were powerful and wealthy men who ruled over smaller regions. Later, some magnates became kings. They had power over larger areas and more people.

FUN FACT

" Harald was nicknamed "Bluetooth" because one of his teeth looked dark blue or black! "

Harald Bluetooth.[40]

Harald became a Christian around 965 CE. He helped spread the new religion across Denmark. He even had large stones carved to show that he and his people had become Christian. These stones were called the Jelling stones.

Harald Bluetooth helped unite the people of Denmark. He even tried to convert people in Norway, though not everyone agreed with him. Later Viking rulers had more success spreading the new religion.

After Harald Bluetooth, his son, **Sweyn** (*swayn*) **Forkbeard**, became king. Around 1013 CE, Sweyn and his Viking army invaded England. The English king at the time, **Æthelred** (*eth-uhl-red*), left the country and went to Normandy. Sweyn was declared king of England, but he died shortly after in 1014 CE.

King Canute

Sweyn's son, **Canute** (*can-oot*), became the new Viking king of England in 1016 CE. He also ruled Denmark and Norway. He created what is called the North Sea Empire. Canute ruled England until he died in 1035 CE.

King Canute.[41]

During his rule, the Viking raids mostly stopped. Many Vikings decided to stay in England, marry local people, and live as farmers, traders, and rulers. They no longer needed to raid to support their families.

The Last Viking Invasion

The final Viking attempt to take England came in 1066 CE. The king of Norway, Harald **Hardrada** (*har-drah-dah*), led a huge army into northern England. He had about ten thousand men with him. On September 25th, 1066, at the Battle of Stamford Bridge, the English army defeated the Vikings. Harald Hardrada was killed in the battle.

Harald Hardrada.[42]

FUN **FACT**

" Many historians believe this battle marks the end of the Viking Age. "

Just a few weeks later, another army invaded England. This one was led by Duke William of Normandy. He later became known as William the Conqueror. William was a descendant of the Vikings! He defeated Harold Godwinson at the Battle of Hastings in October 1066.

The Viking raids that had once spread fear across Europe were over.

Chapter 9 Activity

Fill in the blanks below.

1. During the Viking era, people who didn't follow Christianity were known as_____.

2. Harald Gormsson made himself the king of Denmark. His nickname was _____.

3. Many believe that the Viking Age ended with the death of Harald Hardrada at the Battle of _____.

4. By the mid-900s, the practice and beliefs of _____ had spread throughout Europe.

5. William the Conqueror was a descendant of _____.

Chapter 9 Answers

1. Pagans

2. Bluetooth

3. Stamford Bridge

4. Christianity

5. Vikings

Conclusion

The Vikings might have lived over a thousand years ago, but their story is far from forgotten. These brave and bold people changed history with their ships, their raids, their travels, and their curiosity about the world. They were more than just fierce warriors. They were also farmers, sailors, traders, and storytellers.

We still see the Vikings' influence all around us today. Museums hold their tools, jewelry, and weapons. Towns and cities, like Dublin, were founded by Vikings. We read about them in books, see them in movies, and even celebrate their memory in parades and festivals.

From the runes they carved into stone to the stories passed down through the centuries, the Vikings left their mark on the world. They remind us that even in harsh times, people can be strong, curious, and courageous. Their legacy lives on, not just in history books but also in the ways we remember and honor their adventures today.

If you want to learn more about tons of other exciting historical periods, check out our other books!

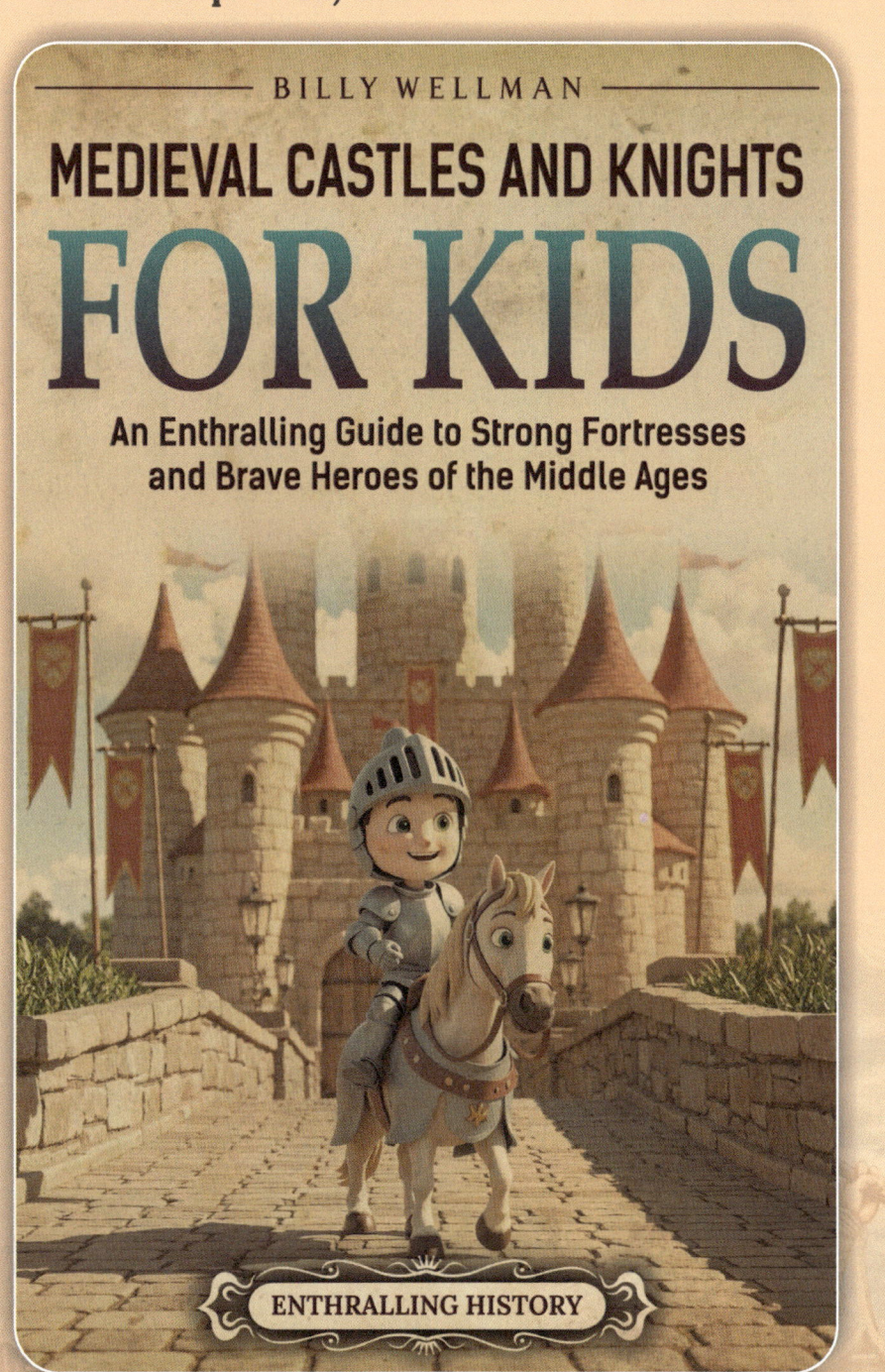

BILLY WELLMAN

MEDIEVAL CASTLES AND KNIGHTS
FOR KIDS

An Enthralling Guide to Strong Fortresses and Brave Heroes of the Middle Ages

ENTHRALLING HISTORY

References

People of the Ancient World: The Vikings. Schomp, Virginia. 2005, Franklin Watts, A Division of Scholastic, Inc., New York.

Life of the Ancient Vikings. Richardson, Hazel. 2005. Crabtree Publishing, New York.

Uncovering History: Everyday Life of the Ancient Vikings. Grant, Neil. 2003, McRae Books, Italy.

Viking Hygiene, Clothing, & Jewelry. https://www.worldhistory.org/article/1840/viking-hygiene-clothing--jewelry/

Follow the Paths of Viking Raiders from Norway to North America. https://www.smithsonianmag.com/travel/visit-viking-settlement-sites-180965257/

Yggdrasil – Yggdrasil. https://www.britannica.com/topic/Yggdrasill

Yggdrasil – Nine Realms of Norse Cosmology. https://www.worldhistory.org/article/1305/nine-realms-of-norse-cosmology/

10 Things You May Not Know About the Vikings. https://www.history.com/news/10-things-you-may-not-know-about-the-vikings

Yale News. The Vikings: Yale Historian looks at the myths vs. the history. https://news.yale.edu/2013/03/08/vikings-yale-historian-looks-myths-vs-history

Women in the Viking Age. Death, Life after Death and Burial Customs. https://www.duo.uio.no/bitstream/handle/10852/26661/Master_Thesis___f%5B1%5D..pdf?sequence=1

Thor's Hammer. https://norse-mythology.org/symbols/thors-hammer/

Lindisfarne Raid. https://www.britannica.com/event/Lindisfarne-Raid

Viking Raids on Paris. https://www.worldhistory.org/Viking_Raids_on_Paris/

Battle of Hafrsfjord. https://www.britannica.com/topic/Battle-of-Hafrsfjord

The Vikings in Iceland. https://www.worldhistory.org/article/1310/the-vikings-in-iceland/#:~:text=According%20to%20the%20Landn%C3%A1mab%C3%B3k%2C%20the%20first%20settler%20in,off%20course%20en%20route%20to%20the%20Faeroe%20Islands.

The Vikings in Norway. https://www.britannica.com/place/Norway/Earliest-peoples#ref188684

Basil II – Byzantine Emperor. https://www.britannica.com/biography/Basil-II#ref126459

The Varangian Guard: Old Norse Elite Viking Warriors. https://vikingr.org/explorers/varangian

Harald Bluetooth & The Conversion of Denmark. https://www.worldhistory.org/article/1733/harald-bluetooth--the-conversion-of-denmark/

Norman Conquest. https://www.britannica.com/event/Norman-Conquest

Image Sources

[1] DemonDays64, CC BY-SA 4.0 <https://creativecommons.org/licenses/by-sa/4.0>, via Wikimedia Commons; https://commons.wikimedia.org/wiki/File:Map_of_Scandinavia.svg

[2] https://commons.wikimedia.org/wiki/File:Christian-krohg-leiv-eriksson.jpg

[3] Grzegorz Wysocki, CC BY 3.0 <https://creativecommons.org/licenses/by/3.0>, via Wikimedia Commons, https://commons.wikimedia.org/wiki/File:Exhibition_in_Viking_Ship_Museum,_Oslo_01.jpg

[4] NTNU Vitenskapsmuseet, CC BY 2.0 <https://creativecommons.org/licenses/by/2.0>, via Wikimedia Commons, https://commons.wikimedia.org/wiki/File:Gjermundbu_helmet_-_cropped.jpg

[5] Wolfmann, CC BY-SA 4.0 <https://creativecommons.org/licenses/by-sa/4.0>, via Wikimedia Commons; https://commons.wikimedia.org/wiki/File:Cultural_History_(historisk)_Museum_Oslo._VIKINGR_Norwegian_Viking-Age_Exhibition_11_Elaborate_swords,_decorated_hilts,_ornated_blades,_home-forged_and_foreign-made,_ca_800-1000._Found_in_Telemark,_Nordland,_Hedmark._4706.jpg

[6] Berig, CC BY-SA 3.0 <https://creativecommons.org/licenses/by-sa/3.0>, via Wikimedia Commons; https://commons.wikimedia.org/wiki/File:Hammars_(I).JPG

[7] https://commons.wikimedia.org/wiki/File:Gamla_Uppsala_-_line_of_tumuli.jpg

[8] Berig, CC BY 3.0 <https://creativecommons.org/licenses/by/3.0>, via Wikimedia Commons; https://commons.wikimedia.org/wiki/File:S%C3%B6_65,_Djulefors.jpg

[9] Photographer Roberto Fortuna, commissioned by the Danish National Museum, CC BY-SA 3.0 <https://creativecommons.org/licenses/by-sa/3.0>, via Wikimedia Commons; https://commons.wikimedia.org/wiki/File:Jellingsten_stor_2.jpg

[10] Wolfmann, CC BY-SA 4.0 <https://creativecommons.org/licenses/by-sa/4.0>, via Wikimedia Commons; https://commons.wikimedia.org/wiki/File:Vikings_costumes_woman_man_Arkeologisk_museum_Stavanger,_Norway_2015-05-27.jpg

[11] Wolfgang Sauber, CC BY-SA 3.0 <https://creativecommons.org/licenses/by-sa/3.0>, via Wikimedia Commons; https://commons.wikimedia.org/wiki/File:Fornsalen_-_Silberschatz_von_Spelling.jpg

[12] Frank Vincentz, CC BY-SA 3.0 <https://creativecommons.org/licenses/by-sa/3.0>, via Wikimedia Commons; https://commons.wikimedia.org/wiki/File:Busdorf_-_Haithabu_-_Wikinger-H%C3%A4user_05_ies.jpg

[13] Julia Velkova, CC BY 2.0 <https://creativecommons.org/licenses/by/2.0>, via Wikimedia Commons; https://commons.wikimedia.org/wiki/File:Viking_village.jpg

[14] Own work, CC BY-SA 3.0 <http://creativecommons.org/licenses/by-sa/3.0/>, via Wikimedia Commons; https://commons.wikimedia.org/wiki/File:Viking_swords.jpg

[15] https://commons.wikimedia.org/wiki/File:Lathgertha_by_Morris_Meredith_Williams.png

[16] https://commons.wikimedia.org/wiki/File:The_Ash_Yggdrasil_by_Friedrich_Wilhelm_Heine.jpg

[17] https://commons.wikimedia.org/wiki/File:Odhin.png

[18] https://commons.wikimedia.org/wiki/File:M%C3%A5rten_Eskil_Winge_-_Tor%27s_Fight_with_the_Giants_-_Google_Art_Project.jpg

[19] https://commons.wikimedia.org/wiki/File:Freya_by_Johannes_Gehrts.jpg

[20] https://commons.wikimedia.org/wiki/File:Detail_from_G_181.jpg

[21] Kim Traynor, CC BY-SA 3.0 <https://creativecommons.org/licenses/by-sa/3.0>, via Wikimedia Commons; https://commons.wikimedia.org/wiki/File:Lindisfarne_Priory_ruins_and_St._Aidan_statue.jpg

[22] https://commons.wikimedia.org/wiki/File:Viking_Expansion.svg

[23] Balou46, CC BY-SA 4.0 <https://creativecommons.org/licenses/by-sa/4.0>, via Wikimedia Commons; https://commons.wikimedia.org/wiki/File:NO-vikingskiphuset-oseberg-05.jpg

[24] http://en.wikipedia.org/wiki/File:Viking_Siege_of_Paris.jpg

[25] https://commons.wikimedia.org/wiki/File:Ole_Peter_Hansen_Balling_Harald_H%C3%A5rfagre_i_slaget_ved_Hafrsfjord.jpg

[26] Wolfmann, CC BY-SA 4.0 <https://creativecommons.org/licenses/by-sa/4.0>, via Wikimedia Commons; https://commons.wikimedia.org/wiki/File:Cultural_History_(historisk)_Museum_Oslo_VIKINGR_Norwegian_Viking-Age_Exhib_02_Hon_Hoard_(Hoenskatten)_Gold_treasure_875-900_(1)_Neck_arm_rings_Frankish_jewelry_Arabian_coins_w_loops_Necklace_glass_beads_Roman_gemstone_English_ring_619.jpg

[27] Sven Rosborn, CC BY-SA 3.0 <http://creativecommons.org/licenses/by-sa/3.0/>, via Wikimedia Commons; https://commons.wikimedia.org/wiki/File:Viking_towns_of_Scandinavia_2.jpg

[28] Petter Ulleland, CC BY-SA 4.0 <https://creativecommons.org/licenses/by-sa/4.0>, via Wikimedia Commons; https://commons.wikimedia.org/wiki/File:Osebergskipet_2016.jpg

[29] Hel-hama, CC BY-SA 3.0 <https://creativecommons.org/licenses/by-sa/3.0>, via Wikimedia Commons; https://commons.wikimedia.org/wiki/File:England_878.svg

[30] Hel-hama, CC BY-SA 3.0 <https://creativecommons.org/licenses/by-sa/3.0>, via Wikimedia Commons; https://commons.wikimedia.org/wiki/File:England_Great_Army_map.svg

[31] en:User:Bogdangiusca, CC BY-SA 3.0 <http://creativecommons.org/licenses/by-sa/3.0/>, via Wikimedia Commons; https://commons.wikimedia.org/wiki/File:Vikings-Voyages.png

[32] Imars: Michael Shea., CC BY-SA 2.5 <https://creativecommons.org/licenses/by-sa/2.5>, via Wikimedia Commons; https://commons.wikimedia.org/wiki/File:Rollo_statue_in_falaise.JPG

[33] SeikoEn, CC BY-SA 3.0 <http://creativecommons.org/licenses/by-sa/3.0/>, via Wikimedia Commons;

https://commons.wikimedia.org/wiki/File:East_Slavic_tribes_peoples_8th_9th_century.jpg

[34] https://commons.wikimedia.org/wiki/File:Leif_Erikson_Discovers_America_Hans_Dahl.jpg

[35] https://commons.wikimedia.org/wiki/File:%D0%92%D0%B0%D1%80%D1%8F%D0%B3%D0%B8.jpg

[36] https://commons.wikimedia.org/wiki/File:The_body_of_Leo_V_is_dragged_to_the_Hippodrome_through_the_Skyla_Gate.jpg

[37] https://commons.wikimedia.org/wiki/File:Hagia-sofia-viking.jpg

[38] Venetian Arsenal, CC BY-SA 4.0 <https://creativecommons.org/licenses/by-sa/4.0>, via Wikimedia Commons; https://commons.wikimedia.org/wiki/File:Arsenale_(Venice)_-_First_Ancient_Greek_lion.jpg

[39] https://commons.wikimedia.org/wiki/File:Ansgarius_predikar_Christna_l%C3%A4ran_i_Sverige_by_Hugo_Hamilton.jpg

[40] https://commons.wikimedia.org/wiki/File:Harald_Bl%C3%A5tand_(Roskilde_Domkirke).JPG

[41] https://commons.wikimedia.org/wiki/File:Cnut_the_Great_-_MS_Royal_14_B_VI.jpg

[42] Colin Smith / Harald Hardrada – CC BY-SA 2.0; https://commons.wikimedia.org/wiki/File:Harald_Hardrada_window_in_Kirkwall_Cathedral_geograph_2068881.jpg

Printed in Dunstable, United Kingdom